JAMIE ARMITAGE

An Interrogation is Jamie Armitage's debut play. It opened at Summerhall, Edinburgh in August 2023, where it enjoyed an award-winning, sold-out run.

Jamie is co-director of *SIX: The Musical*, which is currently playing in the West End, on Broadway, and multiple other locations worldwide. For his work on *SIX* he was nominated for a Tony Award for Best Direction of a Musical.

Other directing credits include *The Red and the Black* (Tokyo Metropolitan Theatre); *Straight Line Crazy* (The Shed; co-directed with Nicholas Hytner); *Southern Belles: A Tennessee Williams Double Bill* (King's Head Theatre); *Spring Awakening* and *Sweeney Todd* (RCSSD); *And Tell Sad Stories of the Death of Queens* (King's Head Theatre); *Love Me Now* (Tristan Bates Theatre).

He is an Associate Director of the Bridge Theatre. He was a resident director at the Almeida Theatre from 2019 to 2021, and an associate artist at the King's Head Theatre.

Jamie Armitage

AN
INTERROGATION

NICK HERN BOOKS

London

www.nickhernbooks.co.uk

For André

An Interrogation was first produced by Ellie Keel Productions and performed at Summerhall, Edinburgh, during the Edinburgh Festival Fringe on 1 August 2023, with the following cast:

RUTH PALMER	Bethan Cullinane
CAMERON ANDREWS	Jamie Ballard
JOHN CULIN	John Macneill

It transferred to Hampstead Theatre Downstairs, London, on 16 January 2025, with the following cast:

RUTH PALMER	Rosie Sheehy
CAMERON ANDREWS	Jamie Ballard
JOHN CULIN	Colm Gormley

Writer and Director	Jamie Armitage
Designer	Sarah Mercade
Lighting Designer	Jonathan Chan
Sound Designer	Tom Foskett Barnes
Video Designer	Dan Light
Casting Director	Becky Paris
Stage Manager	Aime Neeme
Production Manager	Josh Collins
Executive Producer	Ellie Keel
Deputy Producer	Natasha Ketel

An Interrogation is based on Jim Smyth's interview with Russell Williams (7 February 2010).

Characters

RUTH PALMER, *mid-twenties to early thirties. An ambitious,*
headstrong detective
CAMERON ANDREWS, *forties to fifties. A well-dressed,*
charming and seemingly respectable man
JOHN CULIN, *fifties. Ruth's boss and the Senior Investigating*
Officer for the case

Setting

The story is set in a single interview room in a police station.

The play uses a number of cameras with live footage visible
to the audience. The first is the most functional, an overhead
camera which captures a wide-shot of the entire space. This
is the camera that in the world of the play is recording the
interview and so the footage reflects that with a grainy quality.
It is the default view through the majority of the show.

The other four cameras are not of the world of the play and are
used to alter the audience's perception of a moment, or reveal
information which is hidden to the characters:

i)   A single shot of the interviewer, Ruth.

ii) A single shot on the interviewee, Cameron.

iii) One is concealed under the table pointing at Ruth's knees.

iv) Another concealed under the table pointing at Cameron's
     knees.

Potential shots are marked in the stage directions and are an
offer of possible ways of presenting certain moments.

This text went to press before the end of rehearsals and so may
differ slightly from the play as performed.

Sound: a persistent ticking.

On screen: 'The life expectancy of a person who has been abducted and abandoned is 72 hours.'

Then: '5.38 p.m. Sunday 25th February 2018.'

Finally: 'Joanna Nelson has been missing for over 68 hours.'

Lights up: a plain room in a police station. The room is deliberately nondescript but shows evidence of damage over the years: damp marks on the wall, chipped paint, underfunding. There is a table with three chairs. On the ceiling, a CCTV camera is visible. On the far side of the room from the door is a water cooler.

As the lights shift, the ticking fades and we hear a hype-up pop song play through the speakers. As the lyrics start, RUTH PALMER *enters with headphones in and holding a coffee cup. The music shifts to a quieter level to show it is coming from her headphones. She is mouthing the lyrics to herself in a focused, non-performative way.*

JOHN CULIN *barges in.*

JOHN	He's here.
	RUTH *doesn't hear him.*
	Ruth?
RUTH	Yes, gu–
	RUTH *turns quickly, spills her coffee.*
	Shit.
	Music cuts out as she pauses it.
	Yes, guv?
JOHN	Your guy's here.

RUTH	Great.
JOHN	Getting in the zone?
RUTH	Um, yep. Mindfulness.
JOHN	Really?
RUTH	Rain noises. Helps – get in the – zone.
JOHN	That so?

Both hold a straight face for a beat, then laugh.

Ruth, for a detective you're a really terrible liar.

JOHN *hands her a tissue.*

RUTH	(*Wiping her shirt.*) Well, that's why I'm on our side of the table.
JOHN	Your hand always does that little twitch.
RUTH	It does not.
JOHN	We should get you round for a poker night and I'll rinse you dry with that bluffing.
RUTH	You never know, I might surprise you.

She finishes wiping her shirt.

He's...?

JOHN	Just got here. About to go through the scanners.

RUTH *looks at her watch.*

They're going as fast as they can.

RUTH	(*Anxious grunt.*) Hm.
JOHN	You trust us, trust the team, right?
RUTH	Yes.
JOHN	To the core?

RUTH   Dyed blue through and through.

JOHN   And that's why you're headed to the top.

              RUTH *smiles*.

              But before you inevitably end up outranking
              me, listen to an old hand, and breathe for two
              seconds.

              RUTH *exhales, trying to calm herself.*

              Doesn't exactly look the type.

RUTH   They can't all be dirty creeps in sticky
              waterproofs. He's our guy, I'm sure of it.

JOHN   Hope so. You know I got a letter through this
              morning from that twat of an MP asking us to
              give this 'our closest attention'.

RUTH   You're kidding.

JOHN   Look – (*Hands* RUTH *the white envelope.*)
              Not even addressed. Handed in.

RUTH   (*As she scans the letter.*) Such. A. Smug.
              Little. Man. Maybe don't keep cutting our
              budget and we'd already have found her.

              RUTH *puts the white envelope in her folder.*

JOHN   Handed in. You'd think he would have better
              things to do than waltzing down here.

RUTH   Public appearances.

JOHN   All that matters. Everything set up?

RUTH   Checked it twice.

              RUTH *presses a button on the desk, it turns
              on the projected image of the live-feed from
              the camera above them.*

              It's ready to go.

RUTH *presses the button again; the screens go blank.*

I've got our questions, here. Do you wanna take lead on these first ones and then I'll –

JOHN   I've been thinking, and I'm actually gonna sit this one out.

RUTH   Wha– John, but why?

JOHN   I'll be down the corridor watching on the screens with everyone else, but I think you're ready to take charge of this one.

RUTH   …I'm not sure…

JOHN   You prepped all this, right?

RUTH   Yeah.

JOHN   You don't need me stepping on your toes.

RUTH   But couldn't you just sit in?

JOHN   Ruth. You're my top interviewer, and you've got this. I wouldn't be stepping back if I thought you didn't. And he's your hunch, isn't he?

RUTH   True.

JOHN   I'd just get in your way.

        Beat.

RUTH   You do think it's him, don't you?

JOHN   It's worth us talking to him, yeah.

RUTH   Okay.

        She glances at her watch again.

JOHN   I know you're feeling the clock. We all are. But this is a voluntary. You're gonna have to take your –

RUTH	I know.
JOHN	If you spook him and he walks out, then we can't cross him off –
RUTH	I know.
JOHN	Light touch. You could try the rookie routine.
RUTH	Is that what'll get a posh prick like him to open up?
JOHN	Without a doubt.
RUTH	I think I'm beyond the rookie routine now.
JOHN	It'll get his guard down. Keep your eyes peeled. Find the soft spot. Then nail him.
RUTH	Maybe. Can you see if –
JOHN	Sure, sure – I'll go and hurry him through.
	JOHN *turns to go, then:*
	You good?
RUTH	Yep, yep
	RUTH *presses a hand to her temples.* JOHN *spots her engagement ring.*
JOHN	You're still wearing your ring?
RUTH	Oh, um.
JOHN	I thought you and Mikey…
RUTH	We did.
JOHN	Then why… (*Indicating her engagement ring.*)
RUTH	Appearances, I guess.
JOHN	Hm. Probably best to take it off. Never a good idea to give them something personal to talk about. Remember, softly, softly, eyes peeled, then–

He mimes throwing a little punch to make his point.

RUTH   Yep.

JOHN   Ready?

RUTH   Yes.

JOHN winks and exits. RUTH tries to take her ring off, but she struggles to loosen it. Knock on the door. RUTH swears silently. The ring comes free. She stands, smoothes her shirt then opens the door.

JOHN shows in CAMERON ANDREWS. He appears very calm and composed. JOHN smiles at RUTH before exiting. RUTH is transformed. Her nervous energy is buried and she seems at ease.

Hi Cameron? I'm DC Ruth Palmer.

CAMERON   A pleasure.

RUTH   Can I get you anything? We've got water, but I can get you a coffee or tea or…

CAMERON   How's the coffee?

RUTH   Nearly drinkable.

CAMERON   Is that why some ended up on your shirt?

RUTH   Oh. I thought I – (*Rubs at the stain.*) Some guy in the corridor knocked into me.

CAMERON   Really?

Beat.

RUTH   Yep.

Beat.

CAMERON   How clumsy of him…

Beat.

I'm fine with water, thanks.

RUTH *takes her seat, eyes fixed on* CAMERON, *but the conversation is curiously light and friendly given the situation.*

RUTH   First, I just want to say thank you so much for coming in on a Sunday. I hope we haven't disturbed your day too much?

CAMERON   No, no. Just doing the good-son routine.

RUTH   Oh?

CAMERON   Cooking dinner for my mother.

RUTH   Ah I'm sorry to have dragged –

CAMERON   Not at all. I said I'd be straight back once I've finished up here. Won't be too long will we?

RUTH   Should be quite quick.

CAMERON   I've got about half an hour, is that okay?

RUTH   Should be.

CAMERON   Otherwise many burnt potatoes and one irate mother.

RUTH   This is just what we call a routine investigative conversation. Have you ever been interviewed by the police in a room like this before?

CAMERON   No. Well, once actually. A few years ago. I was getting vetted for high-level security clearance.

RUTH   Really?

CAMERON   I occasionally advise at the Exchequer. But no, I've never spoken to the police in this kind of context.

RUTH   I'm just going to start the camera. We record
                every interview we do. Even small-scale,
                routine ones like this. It's mainly to save you
                having to come back again –

CAMERON   Completely understood. You record away.

                RUTH *presses the record button.*

                *Camera: the grainy overhead shot of the
                room.*

RUTH   I am DC Ruth Palmer and the time is five
                forty-three p.m. on Sunday twenty-fifth
                February 2018. I am here with...

CAMERON   Cameron Andrews. All very formal, isn't it?

RUTH   Always is. It's the same procedure and
                caution that we need to do at the beginning of
                all these interviews, it's –

CAMERON   Fire away.

RUTH   Yep, so – you do not have to say anything
                but it may harm your defence if you do not
                mention when questioned –

CAMERON   Do they make you memorise that at police
                school?

RUTH   Oh yeah, it's like the first lesson – questioned
                something which you later rely on in court.
                Anything you do say may be given in
                evidence. To be clear this is a voluntary
                interview and you are here of your own free
                will, is that correct?

CAMERON   (*Bemused.*) That is correct.

RUTH   Right, um, as this is voluntary, you may leave
                at any time.

CAMERON   Noted.

RUTH   And you are welcome to have a lawyer if you so wish, and one can be provi–

CAMERON   No, no. When you work alongside them as often as I do then you tend to avoid their company as much as possible.

RUTH   Well, if at any moment you want one, just let me know and we can provide a list of options.

CAMERON   That really won't be necessary.

RUTH   Sorry for all those formalities. This really is more of a conversation than anything too serious.

CAMERON   An investigative chat?

RUTH   Yep, ha, yep. It's quite informal. I'll just be asking a few questions.

CAMERON   Can I ask questions too?

                Camera: single of CAMERON.

RUTH   About?

CAMERON   All this. You. Your work… Anything.

RUTH   Um…

CAMERON   It's just all quite interesting.

RUTH   Sure. Sure you can.

                Silence.

CAMERON   I haven't got anything to ask yet but it's nice to know I can if anything springs to mind.

                Camera: overhead shot.

RUTH   Right, um, thank you for coming in on a Sunday. You were coming from your mum's you said.

CAMERON	Not far from here actually, she moved a few months ago. Up near Lambourn so not too arduous a drive.
RUTH	Nice place?
CAMERON	Stunning.
RUTH	Lots of trips down from London then?
CAMERON	Oh yeah, always nice to escape my little bachelor bolt-hole.
RUTH	In Notting Hill?
CAMERON	That's right. Happy to help her though as, despite her claims, she's not really safe to drive herself about which makes the whole moving-house process tricky. I've been playing chauffeur.
RUTH	Ah, I had to do that for my dad when he had a knee op. Made my car feel like a taxi.
CAMERON	I'm not even allowed to use my own car. She insists I drive her around in her battered old Volvo.
RUTH	No?
CAMERON	Oh yeah. And she hates that I'm driving *her* car, but she loathes my Mercedes even more. Too flash, gauche.
RUTH	So –
CAMERON	Proper question time?
RUTH	Something like that. Just to start off, we asked you in today, Cameron, to help with an ongoing investigative matter of two linked cases. The first is Vicky Edwards' death last November. She used to work with you –
CAMERON	At my company, yeah.
RUTH	Exactly. And the second is Joanna Nelson, who –

CAMERON	I think I read about her?
RUTH	You did?
CAMERON	Yeah. She vanished right?
RUTH	Seems so. Joanna disappeared from her house in Streatley a few days ago and hasn't been seen or heard from since then.
CAMERON	God. That's – terrible. How's – uh, how's her family?
	Camera: single of CAMERON.
RUTH	Sorry?
CAMERON	How's her family doing?
RUTH	They're worried. Devastated, um –
CAMERON	Of course. I can only imagine the pain it must be causing them.
RUTH	But, hopeful. They're allowing themselves to hope.
CAMERON	Are you hopeful too?
	Beat.
RUTH	Yes, I am.
	Camera: cut to overhead shot.
CAMERON	And this is linked to Vicky?
RUTH	We certainly believe so. There's a number of similarities between the cases. Similar area. Similar age. Living alone. Same method of forced entry into their houses.
CAMERON	How horrible.
RUTH	So you see the reason for our urgency here. Vicky's autopsy indicated that after her disappearance, she may have been kept alive for a day or two before she was asphyxiated. So if, as we believe, Joanna's disappearance is linked to Vicky's then we're working with

the hope that we may still be able to save her. Obviously the more time that passes the likelihood fades, but –

CAMERON   Is that why you're so tense?

Camera: single of RUTH.

Beat.

RUTH   What?

CAMERON   You've been on edge since we started talking. I wondered if that was why?

RUTH   Um, yep, yep. It's been tough.

CAMERON   I'm sorry to hear that.

Camera: overhead shot.

RUTH   We've been going over every possible lead, no matter how small.

CAMERON   I don't know if I can really be any help.

RUTH   Why not?

CAMERON   I would like to, of course, but I'm not sure how much use I'll really be to you.

Beat.

Camera: single of RUTH.

RUTH   To tell you the truth, I haven't done many of these before.

CAMERON   Really?

RUTH   Yep.

CAMERON   You haven't done many of these before?

RUTH   No. I'm kind of a rookie at this. Only joined a couple of weeks ago.

Beat.

CAMERON	Then why are you doing it by yourself?
	Camera: below the table, RUTH*'s finger tapping on her knee.*
RUTH	Hm?
CAMERON	If you're inexperienced, shouldn't you have someone with you?
RUTH	Ha, yeah probably, but this is a big case. And everyone on the team is talking to potential leads from our top guys all the way down to me, with you.
CAMERON	With me?
RUTH	I meant you as a – low-priority interviewee.
CAMERON	And that's why it's you?
RUTH	Yep. Earning my stripes with a more – straight-forward investigative – chat. Info gathering.
CAMERON	When I got the call to come in for this, I expected one of those big 'tough-talking, no-shit' kind of guys.
RUTH	Oh we have that type too.
CAMERON	Well, I feel much more at ease with a You type. And I'm happy to help in any way I can.
RUTH	I appreciate that.
CAMERON	If I can.
RUTH	Yeah.
	Moment, then –
	Camera: overhead shot.
CAMERON	So. How can I be of assistance?
RUTH	I want to get a clearer image of Vicky, especially in relation to her work. What was she like as an employee?

CAMERON	Well, she was – brilliant, hard-working, a real asset to the company.
RUTH	And your company is management related, correct?
CAMERON	Yeah, we 'help clients achieve operational excellence by sharpening their competitive edge' which is our shiny way of saying we get companies to run better.
RUTH	Cutting jobs?
CAMERON	Restructuring and sometimes implementing reductions, yes.
RUTH	And that's the work you've been doing at the Exchequer?
CAMERON	Advising there on all the – savings they're doing.
RUTH	Right, okay.
CAMERON	Sorry, but how is this…
RUTH	Just background. For Vicky. Did you know her particularly well?
CAMERON	You know what, I can't say I ever did. She was just a junior manager's assistant, so our paths didn't really…
RUTH	But she worked for you?
CAMERON	Yes, only indirectly though. Large companies are like that. I mean, do you know all your bosses?
RUTH	I know them, yes.
CAMERON	But they don't necessarily know you?
RUTH	Uh, no.
CAMERON	I mean that guy who showed me in, he certainly knows you.

RUTH	John? Well yeah, we're close.
CAMERON	Seemed so.
	Beat.
RUTH	– yep, but – Vicky, you had met her?
CAMERON	I had, yes.
RUTH	Okay.
CAMERON	But only once, perhaps. When she joined. I try to make a point of saying hello to all new employees. Show face. Make them feel welcome. Get a look at them. So that would have been early last year. But after that I doubt if we spoke many times, if at all before... November.
RUTH	Do you remember when you first learned about Vicky's death?
CAMERON	It was – um – it was late one night, I got a call about it, well, a voicemail first. I missed the call because I was at this event.
RUTH	An event?
CAMERON	For a charity I run. I set it up actually.
RUTH	Oh?
CAMERON	To help children and adults who sustain head injuries. Learn new skills. My godson was involved in an accident and I wanted to – I don't mean to bore you with this.
RUTH	That sounds – like a very good thing.
CAMERON	Thank you. Well, I was at this performance they put on. Everyone shows the skills they've been learning. It's – I find it deeply inspiring. And after, I checked my phone and saw I had all these missed calls. I knew something was wrong, but not... I called back and found out.

RUTH   What was your reaction?

CAMERON   I – I – couldn't believe it. I was horrified.
              It's always someone else, isn't? An attack
              or death or – it always happens to someone
              away from you. So when it's someone you
              know, even indirectly. When it's that close –
              you just never expect it. Especially...

              Camera: single of CAMERON.

RUTH   Especially?

CAMERON   Especially when she died the way she did,
              getting...

RUTH   Choked with a rope, yep.

CAMERON   Yeah.

RUTH   That must have been quite a shock?

CAMERON   Yeah, yeah it was.

              Camera: overhead shot.

RUTH   And, do you remember how you found out
              that Joanna was missing?

CAMERON   I read about it.

RUTH   When would that have been?

CAMERON   Uh, yesterday I think.

RUTH   Where were you?

CAMERON   At my mother's. We were having breakfast.
              I think that's why I thought of the poor girl's
              family. Looking over at my mother and
              imagining Joanna. Joanna and her family.
              How it must be tearing them apart... I mean
              since then her photo's been everywhere, but it
              was yesterday, yesterday morning.

RUTH   Okay. okay. And this Thursday, do you
              remember what you were doing that evening?

CAMERON	Well, I would've left the office around six and drove down here.
RUTH	And was it a memorable evening in any way?
CAMERON	Uh, not exactly memorable I'd say.
RUTH	But can you remember, like, any details?
CAMERON	Well, it was bucketing it down, right? And I think we got a take-away. Yeah, yeah. That was it. My mother wanted me to drive her somewhere but then we thought best not, with the rain, so we ordered in.
RUTH	Nice. What did you order?
CAMERON	No comment
RUTH	…
CAMERON	Ha, sorry I, ha. I've always wanted to say that.
RUTH	Oh. (*Conciliatory laugh.*)
CAMERON	Um, I think we got a curry. There's this place she loves and so we ordered food in.
RUTH	Just you two?
CAMERON	Yeah.
RUTH	And did she treat you, or…?
CAMERON	I think I paid for that one. She always tries, but I insisted.
RUTH	Yeah, my dad can be a bit like that too, so –
CAMERON	So, you know, right?
RUTH	Yep, it's like a constant battle.
CAMERON	Always is.
RUTH	And was that by card?

Camera: single of CAMERON. *He is rubbing his right wrist, ever so slightly.*

CAMERON	Sorry?
RUTH	How you paid. Was it by card?
CAMERON	Um. Yeah, yeah it would have been.
RUTH	Oh great, that's helpful because we can confirm that easily.
CAMERON	Why would you feel the need to confirm that?
RUTH	This Thursday, the twenty-second, was, as I'm sure you know, the evening Joanna Nelson was last seen.
CAMERON	...I didn't know...
RUTH	Wasn't it in the article you read?
CAMERON	I sort of skim-read it, so – the date, Thursday didn't stick
RUTH	Makes sense
	RUTH *smiles*.
	So much of this work, is just checking and crossing people off so we can move past them, you know?
CAMERON	Sure.
RUTH	Because, when there's a situation like this, where one victim worked for you and the missing person lives not far from where you were that evening. You can see the connection?
CAMERON	Well, not really.
RUTH	But you understand how it could look like an odd coincidence?
CAMERON	I suppose you could see it like that.
RUTH	And we wouldn't be doing our jobs if we didn't check carefully and cross you off, so we can move past you, do you see?

CAMERON   I do, yeah, I – uh – do. I suppose, I mean, you could say there's a connection there. And I'd be happy to help you cross me off, as it were.

RUTH   So we can move past you.

CAMERON   Yeah.

Camera: overhead shot.

RUTH   What did you do with the rest of the evening?

CAMERON   Well, we – I'm trying to remember here – we ate our food, spoke, had a catch-up I mean. Normal dinner.

RUTH   Was it enjoyable?

CAMERON   As much as any meal with one's mother ever is.

RUTH   Okay.

CAMERON   Then I would have gone to bed.

RUTH   What time would that have been?

CAMERON   Maybe nine-thirty, ten. Around then.

RUTH   Is that a normal time for you?

CAMERON   I had this – early-morning call the next day, you see. I wanted an early night so I could be up in time for that.

RUTH   Okay.

CAMERON   International call, so an early start. Before breakfast.

RUTH   Breakfast with Mum?

CAMERON   Yeah.

RUTH   I see.

Silence.

	Cameron. What would you be willing to give me to help us move past you in this investigation...?
CAMERON	Move past me?
RUTH	To overcome the coincidence –
CAMERON	Definitely. Anything. How can I help? What do you need?
RUTH	Samples?
CAMERON	...
RUTH	Only if you're comfortable –
CAMERON	Sure. Absolutely.
RUTH	I know you offered saliva swabs back in –
CAMERON	The whole office did. I thought it was a good gesture of support for the investigation.
RUTH	It was, but now would you be happy to give, y'know, prints...?
CAMERON	Yes.
RUTH	Hair?
CAMERON	Yeah.
RUTH	Footwear impressions?
CAMERON	Um... as in?
RUTH	It's like a scan of your shoe?
CAMERON	...um, yeah, yeah of course. Whatever'll help.
RUTH	You would?
CAMERON	Of course. Anything that – can be of use.
RUTH	Okay, great. That's great. Some sad news, Cameron, I am not actually a forensic specialist, so it won't be me pressing your thumb into the ink.

CAMERON	Ah well.
RUTH	You'll be taken to our team and they'll do those samples. How's that sound?
CAMERON	Okay to me.
RUTH	Great. It's six oh-one p.m. and we are –
CAMERON	Ruth.

Camera: single of CAMERON.

RUTH	Yup.
CAMERON	Can I, I just want to ask – are you going to be discreet about all of this?
RUTH	Discreet?
CAMERON	Well, you see, my company works with some important clients.
RUTH	Okay.
CAMERON	Some very important clients. And I – well, I wouldn't want there to be any rumours about my being brought in for questioning.
RUTH	I understand
CAMERON	– mixed up –
RUTH	Yup.
CAMERON	Because once the rumour mill cranks up, it can be very difficult to stop.
RUTH	Complete discretion. That was part of the reason of inviting you here on a Sunday.
CAMERON	I appreciate that, thank you.

Camera: overhead shot.

RUTH	It's now six oh-two p.m. and we are pausing the interview.

RUTH *presses the button and the screens go blank.*

This shouldn't take too long.

RUTH *smiles, hits the door twice. It opens and* CAMERON *is shown out.* RUTH *retakes her seat. She thinks.*

On screen: '6.03 p.m.: Joanna Nelson missing for nearly 70 hours.'

Time jumps forward as CAMERON *is shown back in.*

How was that?

CAMERON   Inky, (*Waves his ink-stained fingers.*) but fine.

RUTH   The time is six forty-two p.m. This is DC Ruth Palmer and I'm restarting the interview with Cameron Andrews.

CAMERON   That's me.

RUTH   So Cameron, would you mind taking a look at some photos?

CAMERON   Sure.

RUTH   Do you recognise the woman here?

CAMERON   Well, yes. I believe that's the missing woman. Can't recall her name, um…

RUTH   Joanna Nelson, correct. Have you ever seen her before? I mean prior to on the news this weekend.

CAMERON   No. I can't say I ever have.

RUTH   Are you certain?

CAMERON   As much as I can be.

RUTH   Joanna's home in Streatley isn't far from Lambourn, so I wanted to ask. Even if just a small encounter around Streatley or anywhere.

CAMERON	Do people tend to notice strangers in the street?
RUTH	Not everyone, but you seem like someone who – keeps their eyes peeled.
CAMERON	'Eyes peeled', well. Thanks.
RUTH	So. Did you?
CAMERON	I'm certain that I have never seen this woman before.
RUTH	Okay. Okay, now take a look at this photo here. Do you know who this is?
CAMERON	Of course. That's Vicky.
RUTH	Yes. And, you –
CAMERON	Have you taken off a ring?

Camera: single of RUTH.

RUTH	Sorry?
CAMERON	There's an indent on your finger. Looks like you took off a 'special' ring.
RUTH	Um.
CAMERON	Did you?
RUTH	Um, yep I did.
CAMERON	What was it?
RUTH	It was, um, an engagement ring.
CAMERON	Why take it off?
RUTH	Because, well, because it ended.
CAMERON	But you were still wearing it today?
RUTH	Yep, force of habit. But John, my boss, pointed it out and I took it off.
CAMERON	Was that for my sake or his?

RUTH	…neither.
CAMERON	Right.
	Camera: overhead shot.
RUTH	Um, you found out about Vicky's, about her death after an event –
CAMERON	For my charity, yeah.
RUTH	– and could – you go into more – detail about the – next steps your company – took.
CAMERON	Well, I – let me see, we had a meeting about it the next day, the next morning in fact and discussed informing the rest of the company and then –
RUTH	Is that when you sent out the email?
	Camera: single of CAMERON.
CAMERON	The email?
RUTH	The email to your entire office on – November seventeenth.
CAMERON	I didn't send that email.
RUTH	It was sent by the chair of the board. You were a signatory –
CAMERON	– yes –
RUTH	– which told your employees to not communicate with the police about the investigation?
CAMERON	I don't believe that's exactly what was said –
RUTH	'…we request staff respect the delicacy of this situation and for the time being do not communicate with anyone, including – '
CAMERON	Look, I want to be completely clear here, this was discussed at the time and felt to be

	the adequate response given the high-profile nature of some of our clients.
RUTH	Why did you authorise this email?
CAMERON	On reflection, yes maybe, it was not the cleverest move to send it, but that was before we knew the scale of the situation.
RUTH	You knew she'd been murdered...
CAMERON	Well, we didn't actually. We knew she had died but thought it might have been an accident, or suicide. We had no idea what Vicky might have got, got mixed up in.
	CAMERON *rubs his right wrist.*
RUTH	Mixed up in?
CAMERON	Yeah. The police were involved, what were we supposed to think? So we acted to preserve, to protect the company. Which, evidently, was the wrong move once the details of the case became clear. Then we helped.
RUTH	Did you?
CAMERON	Yes.
RUTH	How?
CAMERON	We cooperated. Fully. With the police – the investigation. In any way we could. We volunteered DNA, those saliva swab things. I think that shows a willingness to help, doesn't it?
RUTH	The email though. It just feels like an odd decision to make?
CAMERON	With hindsight. Not at the time.
RUTH	Okay.

CAMERON *smoothes his right sleeve slightly.*

Camera: overhead shot.

This week we've been looking more at Vicky and everyone she worked with, which is why we're chatting today. We've also been looking at the check-ins and check-out times of most of your workforce...

CAMERON   (*Trying to lighten the mood.*) I'd be fascinated to see those myself.

RUTH   I was wondering would you be happy to look over some dates of yours. Just to get a clearer picture of everything?

CAMERON   Sure.

RUTH   So. This Friday and the Friday before you were working from home?

CAMERON   Yes, once, once from my flat and this Friday from my mother's, but I was not in the office those days, no.

RUTH   And this weekend, you stayed with your mum the whole time?

CAMERON   Yeah.

RUTH   So these last seventy-two hours you've been in the Lambourn area?

Camera: single of CAMERON.

CAMERON   Yeah.

RUTH   Okay. And this is November now. Were you still taking Fridays off then?

CAMERON   Usually.

RUTH   Because with the records, it shows you were at the office every Friday bar two...?

CAMERON	That's probably right. I'm not always the best at sticking to my resolutions. Work-life balance. You must know how it is?
RUTH	Yep, I do.
CAMERON	Is that why things ended with – (*Indicates her missing ring.*)
RUTH	Something like that. Back to November. One of those Fridays you also were out of your office the Thursday before it – why was that?
CAMERON	I can't really remember. I'd have to check my diary, or call my –
RUTH	Meetings? Illness?
CAMERON	I can't recall exactly.
RUTH	Not at all?
CAMERON	Probably working from home, or down here at my mother's. But I'd have to check.
RUTH	I ask cos that was when Vicky disappeared.
CAMERON	…what are you driving at here?
	Camera: below the table, RUTH*'s hand on her knee, tapping tensely.*
RUTH	Just trying to get as much information as possible.
CAMERON	Huh.
RUTH	And before we can move past you in this investigation, we have to cross off these – coincidences.
CAMERON	As you said.
	Camera: overhead shot.
RUTH	Yep, so this last Thursday, you said you left at six p.m. but the record shows you leaving before five thirty p.m?
	Camera: single of CAMERON.

CAMERON   What's in half an hour?

RUTH   I looked up how long the journey is from
            your office to your mother's house, and it's
            about ninety minutes or so.

CAMERON   Varies, but yes that's about right.

RUTH   And once more, you said you never
            knew of Joanna before reading about her
            disappearance?

CAMERON   Yes.

RUTH   Never seen her, never met her?

CAMERON   ...yes.

RUTH   Then, why were you in Streatley on Thursday
            evening?

            Silence.

CAMERON   Pardon?

RUTH   Why were you in Streatley this Thursday
            evening?

CAMERON   ...

RUTH   When someone disappears, we gather as
            much information as possible to map their
            last known movements. With Joanna, her
            Thursday was very normal. She was on her
            train home, as normal. Caught the bus, as
            normal. And got off at the bus stop at the top
            of her street, as normal. But then when we
            looked closer at the bus's camera we noticed
            something.

            She pushes a photo across the table towards
            CAMERON.

            It's raining so the picture quality isn't great
            but hopefully you can still make it out.

There it is. A silver Mercedes. Your silver Mercedes. Can you explain that?

Silence.

Cameron. Why were you in Streatley?

CAMERON	…
RUTH	Why?
CAMERON	…
RUTH	I need a proper answer on this one, Cameron. You can't just smile and shrug this off.
CAMERON	…
RUTH	Why were you there?
CAMERON	What time was it?
RUTH	Time?
CAMERON	Yes, what time was it when that photo was taken?
RUTH	Um – (*Looks through notes.*) it was seven oh-nine p.m.
CAMERON	Well, there you are.
RUTH	…
CAMERON	My mother lives in Lambourn. I know you've looked up the route but I imagine you've never driven it yourself, have you?
RUTH	Uh, no.
CAMERON	If you try to drive directly from town you can get stuck in traffic for an hour or more. So I tend to go another route I know, which I believe does go through Streatley. I don't know if you have, but were you to go through all the bus cameras around that area, you'd see that I drove through Streatley last week, the week before and many weeks before that too.

RUTH	Right.
CAMERON	I understand your enthusiasm about this coincidence, DC Palmer, but that's all it is. A coincidence. And one you can confidently cross off.
	Camera: below the table, RUTH*'s jittery hand.*
RUTH	But you see why we needed to ask about that?
CAMERON	Do I?
RUTH	You may have seen – something – anything which might have helped us find out what happened to Joanna.
CAMERON	In case I'd kept my 'eyes peeled'?
RUTH	Yep.
CAMERON	It seemed like you were suggesting I was involved in some way?
RUTH	Not at all, I was just –
	Camera: single of CAMERON.
CAMERON	And for that you need a lot more than my missing a few days of work and happening to drive near her house. Wouldn't you need a close DNA match, or fingerprint evidence? And given that I've provided both of those already and you're still talking to me shows that there evidently hasn't been a match. Has there?
RUTH	Um, it can take –
CAMERON	Or what about the passive data from my phone? You'd just need to look at that and you'll see that I was home all of Thursday night and didn't go anywhere near her house.

	Or my car. Look at the GPS and that will confirm, again, that I didn't leave Lambourn at all that night.
RUTH	That's something we can look at very easily –
CAMERON	I'm really getting tired of this. First, you drag me out on –
RUTH	– you were asked –
CAMERON	– on a Sunday –
RUTH	– not dragged –
CAMERON	Then you give me all this 'help the investigation' schtick, then you start making wild suggestions that I am somehow involved with all this.
RUTH	I'm just trying to find out what –
CAMERON	See, I don't want to tell you how to do your job, but you're looking in the wrong place: I'm not the kind of person who does things like this.
RUTH	You are cos people like you always get away with it.

Silence.

CAMERON *exhales.*

CAMERON   Look, Ruth. I know it's – popular at the moment for people of your generation to hate men who come from my background, and look and speak like I do, but – I'm a good person. I care for my mother, I run a charity. I work hard. And you may not like what my job is but every day I try to do what I believe is best for the world. And I just wish more people of your age could recognise that.

Silence.

May I be excused for a moment?

RUTH   Of course. Do you need anything at –

CAMERON   No, no. Just the bathroom. I'm happy to help
              again in any way I can, but I think we could
              both do with a cool-off before we wrap this
              up.

RUTH   Yep. Someone will accompany you – The
              time is seven oh-two p.m. We are pausing the
              interview to allow Cameron Andrews to go to
              the bathroom.

              RUTH *presses the record button and the
              screens go blank.* CAMERON *is still staring
              at the photos.*

              The bathroom is just down the corridor to the
              right. Someone will escort you to...

              *As she is getting up to open the door, she
              spots* CAMERON*'s expression.*

              Are you okay? Cameron?

CAMERON   (*Looking up from the photos.*) You look a lot
              like them you know.

RUTH   ...

CAMERON   I just, I don't mean to be – But, you do look
              a bit like these two. Sorry... Down to the
              right. Back in a moment, thank you.

              RUTH *opens the door for* CAMERON. *He is
              shown out.*

              RUTH *closes the door and screams into her
              hands.*

              *Screen: 'Joanna Nelson – missing for almost
              71 hrs.'*

              *Then she stops as... a thought clicks into
              place... a smile spreads across her face.*

              JOHN *barges into the room.*

JOHN	What the fuck was that?
RUTH	I've got it.
JOHN	'People like you always get away with it.'
RUTH	That slipped out. But I've got it.
JOHN	And mocking him with that shrug-and-smile stuff.
RUTH	Oh come on.
JOHN	You don't say studenty bullshit like that to a suspect.
RUTH	I know, I messed up I'm – sorry but…
JOHN	Yes you fucking did.
RUTH	I'm – sorry.
	Silence.
JOHN	We've got to let him go.
RUTH	– why?
JOHN	Ruth, you've wasted enough time –
RUTH	No, no. It's him.
JOHN	Look, I know you're in a place right now what with Mikey and the –
RUTH	– that has nothing to do with it.
	Beat.
JOHN	I didn't mean – (*Apologetic-ish shrug.*)
RUTH	(*Quietly.*) I know it's him.
JOHN	You've got nothing.
RUTH	But –
JOHN	Go on. Name one definitive piece of evidence you have.

RUTH	But that's exactly it.
JOHN	If there was a fingerprint, a drop of DNA then sure, but there's nothing. You can't link anyone to being there, let alone him.
RUTH	He knows that though.
JOHN	What?
RUTH	Didn't you hear his outburst at the end? He knows about that kind of evidence, which is why he was careful. And why we can't find anything.
JOHN	You can't make an arrest based on there being no fucking evidence.
RUTH	But –
JOHN	Ruth, you're getting too fixated on him.
RUTH	I just need more time.
JOHN	It's a voluntary. He's already saying he wants to wrap this up.
RUTH	Let's arrest him then.
JOHN	On what evidence?
RUTH	The boot print?
JOHN	Fat chance. Here – (*Hands over two printouts.*) Similar but nothing conclusive. No court would ever give you a warrant based on that.
RUTH	Shit.
JOHN	We need to stop this. Now. It's all getting too personal.
RUTH	It's not.
JOHN	Why were you letting him ask you about your ring, and you and Mikey?

RUTH	I didn't tell him much.
JOHN	You shouldn't be letting him even ask.
RUTH	But I need him to open up. Everything else is just bouncing off him.
JOHN	Let this go. You're wasting time here. Joanna's been missing –
RUTH	I know exactly how fucking long Joanna has been missing for.
	Beat.
JOHN	Good. Then you can see why I'm pulling you out to get you working on something that might help find her.
RUTH	…I… I know it's him though.
JOHN	How? Come on, pretend I'm a judge.
RUTH	John, I don't want to play –
JOHN	No, no. How?
RUTH	– we don't have –
JOHN	Convince me. What do you have that links him to these crimes?
RUTH	Um, so, he was in the area on the night that –
JOHN	His mum lives round there. And he's been down many times when there haven't been murders.
RUTH	Um, right. Uh. The email, asking his employees –
JOHN	A natural response for a nervy CEO. He then cooperated by offering samples.
RUTH	Okay, uh, asking me to be discreet was –
JOHN	Same thing.

RUTH	Uh, we, we can't prove that he did go to bed early on Thursday.
JOHN	What are they more likely to believe: that a guy wanted an early night, or that someone popped out to kidnap a stranger after enjoying a nice vindaloo?
RUTH	Do you even believe what you're saying?
JOHN	I'm just showing you how none of what you said proves anything. And to be honest, watching on the screens, I'm not seeing what you're seeing.
RUTH	But in here – I know.
JOHN	The recording from that camera is what a court will watch and on that, he does not look guilty of anything. A bit too clever for his own good, yeah. A bit shifty, maybe. But that's it.
RUTH	What about when he said that thing when he was looking at the photos? He stared at me and said 'You look a lot like them.'
JOHN	I didn't hear that?
RUTH	It was before he went out just now.
JOHN	Really?
RUTH	Yep.
	Beat.
JOHN	Were you still recording?
RUTH	Uh –
JOHN	Were you?
RUTH	…
JOHN	There you go. Even then… It's a little creepy but – I mean you do look a bit like them both.

	I've thought that before. We all have. But it's not enough to go on.
RUTH	John –
JOHN	You're so certain it's him that everything you see him do just confirms what you already believe.
RUTH	Okay... Okay. Fine. Send him home.
JOHN	It happens to the best of us.
RUTH	...
JOHN	Ruth, I'm as pissed off as you. I hoped this might work. You alone here with him. But it hasn't shown us anything.
RUTH	What do you mean me alone?
JOHN	You know, you, interviewing him. The focus, the pressure of that, might've got him to crack or something, but it hasn't. Has it?

RUTH *shakes her head.*

And you heard all those hints he dropped about his clients? God knows who he's friends with and the trouble that could cause us.

RUTH	That's not a reason to not –
JOHN	I know, I know. I'm not saying it is, but you just need to look at him. Have you ever seen anybody so calm when you suggest he may have murdered someone?
RUTH	But that's why people like him always –
JOHN	– don't start this again –
RUTH	– get away with stuff like this and –
JOHN	Stuff like this?

RUTH	With anything! They don't *seem* like the people who would do that, but they *are*.
JOHN	You know I believe in you, but to anyone else this just sounds like some – some personal-prejudice crusade.
RUTH	No, that's not fair – no, you know the type I'm talking about. They look us in the eyes and say something that is bullshit but we believe them because of the way they smile and, and...
JOHN	Ruth?

RUTH *starts to grab papers from the table and stuffs them into the folder to bulk it out.*

What are you –

RUTH *also puts in the photo of the boot-print.*

Ruth!

RUTH	Twenty minutes.
JOHN	Huh?
RUTH	That's all I need. Twenty minutes.
JOHN	No – I'm not letting you drag this out any...

RUTH *neatens out the now thick folder and places it purposefully on the table.*

Ruth. Stop this.

RUTH	Twenty minutes that's all.
JOHN	No, we need you back with –
RUTH	Come on. If there's nothing after that time, then, then he can go.
JOHN	Ruth...
RUTH	Please. If you believe in me at all. Then, let me.

A knock on the door.

Please.

JOHN   If he asks to leave, he leaves?

RUTH *nods. Both hold for a moment, then* JOHN *opens the door and* CAMERON *is shown in.*

CAMERON   Hi, sorry. I wasn't sure whether I should wait or –

JOHN   It's fine – I'm on my way out.

CAMERON   Oh right, should I –?

JOHN   No, no not at all. Was just popping by to bring DC Palmer some documents.

JOHN *exits.*

CAMERON *appears completely calm and composed again but stays standing for a moment looking at* RUTH.

CAMERON   Are we ready to wrap this up then?

RUTH   Please take a seat.

CAMERON   (*Sitting.*) ...for the last little questions.

RUTH   This is DC Ruth Palmer, the time is seven eleven p.m. and I am recommencing the interview with Cameron Andrews. (*Smiling.*) How are you feeling?

CAMERON   Better, thank you. How about you?

RUTH   Look. I get it. There's something about these rooms, the light, these stupid uncomfortable chairs that just puts people on – edge.

CAMERON   Thank you for being understanding.

RUTH   Of course.

They smile at each other, then sit in silence.

Camera: single of RUTH.

RUTH *studies the folder. The silence*
continues.

CAMERON   Quite the file.

Silence, again. CAMERON *stares at* RUTH
who continues with her reading.

Are we nearly finished here?

Camera: overhead shot.

RUTH   We are actually.

CAMERON   Good.

RUTH   You can get back for dinner with your mum
then?

CAMERON   Absolutely.

RUTH   I wouldn't want to get you into trouble.

CAMERON   She'll be alright about it. I'll get it in the neck
a bit, but nothing unusual in that.

Silence returns. RUTH *looks at the file again.*

Camera: under the table, we see
CAMERON's *left hand rubbing the inside*
of his right wrist, but his face still looks
completely calm.

Ruth?

RUTH   Cameron, I – I actually wanted to thank you
for how you've been today.

You've cooperated with all of this. Answered
my questions. And you've been helpful and
treated me with respect throughout.

CAMERON   I've tried.

RUTH   And so have I, I hope?

CAMERON   Yeah. More or less, yeah.

Camera: overhead shot.

RUTH   But the thing is with this file here, it paints a different picture from the respectful man I've been speaking to for the last hour. And I'm struggling to try and make those two men fit together. Do you see what I mean?

CAMERON   I'm not sure I'm following you here...

RUTH   What I'm offering you now, Cameron, is a chance to take control. To take control of this situation which is slipping away a bit at the moment.

CAMERON   I don't quite see what you're...

Camera: single of RUTH.

RUTH   Could you have a look at this photo?

CAMERON   Sure.

RUTH   Do you know what it is?

CAMERON   It looks a lot like the underside of a shoe.

RUTH   Yep, it's the footwear impression you did earlier. And now, can you have a look at this photo?

She places another photo in front of CAMERON.

Cameron?

CAMERON   ...

RUTH   Do you know what that is?

CAMERON   A footprint in some mud.

RUTH   Yep, that's right. A footprint in some mud. That mud you see there is actually by a window at the back of Joanna Nelson's

house. The window we know was used by
her attacker to break in.

CAMERON   Huh.

Silence, as he stares at the photos.

RUTH   We know it was late that evening as the rain
made the ground soft. So soft that when
Joanna's attacker stepped up to that window,
their foot pressed down. Leaving that. That
footprint.

CAMERON   Right.

RUTH   Why do you think I'm showing you these two
photos?

CAMERON   I don't know.

RUTH   I think you do. Come on. You're a clever
man.

CAMERON   The shoes look different.

RUTH   That's true. Different shoes. And with most
cases that'd be us stumped. But with this
case, we've been given more funding as our
bosses, even our MP has been pushing us
to solve it. So rather than – 'implementing
reductions' – it means we can ask expensive
experts to help us out a bit. Do you know
what an imprint expert is?

CAMERON   ...no.

RUTH   He studies weight distribution and how
different people have different imprints. So
while to our eyes all you and I see are two
different shoes, the imprint expert will be
able to say whether the person who made this
footprint – (*Indicates the first photo.*) also
made this one – (*Points at the second.*)

CAMERON   Huh.

CAMERON *picks up the two photos and studies them closely.*

Camera: overhead shot.

RUTH Now, whatever you say, we've already sent both these images to our expert. So we're waiting for his response but what you can do is help us clear this up faster. Help us find Joanna in time. Can you help, Cameron?

Silence.

If there is an explanation as to why this could have happened, I want to hear it.

Silence.

To make sense of this all.

Silence...

Cameron. Why you were at Joanna Nelson's house on Thursday evening?

CAMERON I don't believe you.

RUTH What?

CAMERON About these – (*Indicating the photos.*) and your magical imprint expert: I don't believe you.

RUTH It – It doesn't matter if you believe me, we've sent both of these –

CAMERON You're not a very good liar, Ruth.

RUTH What has that got to –

CAMERON It was a nice attempt. At a bluff. Very creative. And your trick with the folder was good. Although that would have been more impressive if it wasn't so obvious that you just stuffed it with a random assortment of papers.

RUTH   I – I –

CAMERON   Now I hate to seem like this kind of person,
                but one has to be on occasions. I'm sure
                my friend at the Exchequer will be very
                impressed when he hears about the activist
                detective who tries to frame innocent people
                with nothing more than bluff, and her class
                prejudice.

RUTH   But –

CAMERON   Because that's all it is. And if that's the
                simplistic way you want to view the world,
                fine. But I'm tired of it now. I'd rather let
                your boss deal with all your – anxieties.
                I, however, would like to leave.

RUTH   You – can't.

CAMERON   Really?

RUTH   …

CAMERON   I believe you said this was a voluntary
                interview, DC Palmer –

RUTH   – yep, but –

CAMERON   – and I would like to be shown out.

RUTH   …

CAMERON   Will you do that?

RUTH   …

CAMERON   Alright. Well then, I think I remember where
                the exit was.

                CAMERON *gets up and crosses to the door.*

RUTH   (*Almost inaudible.*) I – um…

                CAMERON *turns.*

CAMERON   Pardon?

RUTH's right finger taps. She stills it with her left hand and puts her hands out of sight under the table.

Camera: RUTH's *tapping finger on her leg.*

RUTH   My dad used to work as a security guard. And since I was little, he always pushed and pushed me to try for the Force. Sport, curfews, meal plans – for years. And when I got in? I'd never seen him look so happy before.

RUTH takes the ring from her pocket.

My dad loved when his detective daughter started dating another officer. And when Mikey proposed? He kept pushing us to pick a date. And I know he was just proud but it was – suffocating and I didn't know if it was what I wanted – Or...

CAMERON   What did you do?

RUTH   I ended it. With Mikey. And the crushed look on my dad's face when I told him.

CAMERON   ...

RUTH   So. What about you?

CAMERON   Me?

RUTH   Is this how you pictured your life? A successful, rich man like you spending every weekend looking after your ageing mother?

CAMERON   It doesn't –

RUTH   Must be a lot.

CAMERON   I actually enjoy it.

RUTH   How much have you given up for her?

CAMERON   I don't think about it in those terms.

RUTH	Do you find it difficult to be in her company?
CAMERON	No.
RUTH	I asked you earlier if your dinner with her was enjoyable and you said, 'as much as any meal with one's mother is'.
CAMERON	That's not what I meant.
RUTH	Do you find her suffocating?
CAMERON	No.
RUTH	Have you ever done anything to get back at her?
CAMERON	No.
RUTH	Anything to try and give yourself a sense of control?
CAMERON	Stop it.
RUTH	Nothing to feel strong and powerful?
CAMERON	No.
RUTH	Do you resent her domination over you?
CAMERON	For Fuck's Sake, NO!

It's the first time CAMERON's raised his voice. It's like a mask has slipped.

The moment hangs.

RUTH	The morning after. Did what you'd done make breakfast with your mum more bearable? Was having breakfast with your mother more bearable after abducting Joanna?
CAMERON	I don't know what you're talking about.

Silence.

RUTH	Take a seat, Cameron.

CAMERON	No, I'm leaving –
RUTH	You were right about the folder by the way. It's random bits of paper stuffed together. None of the evidence we have is enough to convict you. But we do have enough to submit to a court. And that's what this is, this letter.

Places the white envelope from earlier on the table in front of CAMERON *her fingers tap on it gently.*

	Do you know what's inside?
CAMERON	No.
RUTH	It's a request. For a search warrant. For your mother's house.
CAMERON	…why would you look there?
RUTH	To see if there is anything that can help us find Joanna.
CAMERON	There's nothing there.
RUTH	There could be.
CAMERON	Why would you disturb her about… There's nothing there.
RUTH	We have to be certain though. Be thorough. Just to be sure that there's nothing in your mother's house that could help us find Joanna.

Silence.

CAMERON	It's difficult to believe this is actually happening to me.
RUTH	Why's that?
CAMERON	It just, it just is.

Silence.

RUTH   If you walk out now, this – (*Indicates letter.*) is our only choice?

                CAMERON *shifts, then goes and sits back down.*

                What's on your mind, Cameron? What are you, what are you thinking about?

                Silence.

CAMERON   I'm thinking about what my mother will say when her house is torn up.

RUTH   Okay.

CAMERON   Unnecessarily.

RUTH   You know we don't want that. I don't want to disturb your mum at all. I just want to find Joanna. Can you help me do that?

CAMERON   She loves that house. It's everything to her.

RUTH   I get that, but we need to find Joanna. For her family's sake.

CAMERON   It's not me.

RUTH   …

CAMERON   It's not me.

RUTH   …Cameron…

CAMERON   You may not like —

RUTH   It's not about liking you —

CAMERON   But —

RUTH   You can help us.

CAMERON   I can't.

RUTH   I believe you can.

CAMERON   No matter what you imagine or want to believe, I have —

RUTH	An alibi?
CAMERON	Yeah.
RUTH	The one you told me earlier.
CAMERON	Yes.
RUTH	I thought you had one too. For a sec. Buying dinner, leaving a trace. All checkable, very clever.

Camera: under the table, CAMERON *rubbing his right wrist.*

But then you told me to look at the passive data on your phone, the GPS record of your car.

CAMERON	As it would show I was at my mother's house.
RUTH	It'd only show your phone and your car were there, not you. Felt a bit neat. And you were right, we'd have checked your Mercedes and seen that it had stayed at your mum's all night and you would have been in the clear. But there was something about your confidence. Made me think you might have driven something else, maybe 'some battered old Volvo'? Cos that's what you did, isn't it – you used your mum's car?
CAMERON	I don't know what you're talking about.
RUTH	And the rest of your story? Playing the good son, having curry with Mum –
CAMERON	That's what happened.
RUTH	I'm sure it is but Joanna didn't disappear until much later in the evening. So your story hinges on one thing, will your mum confirm that you definitely stayed in all night? Would she say that you never went out again afterwards?

CAMERON   (*Looking directly at her.*) Yes.

Camera: single of RUTH.

RUTH   I'd have to ask her myself though. In a room like this. This light, that uncomfortable chair. And I'd show her photos. From Vicky's autopsy. Her face. The bruises. The rope burns on her neck. So that as we go over every detail about your movements that night, your mother will have to look at the photos of what you did.

Silence. He is drooped forward. His head down, hands under the table.

Do you trust that she'll still support your story?

CAMERON   ...

RUTH   Do you, Cameron?

Silence.

Eventually, CAMERON *looks up at her.*

Silence. Then –

CAMERON   Please... call me Cam.

RUTH   Okay.

Silence.

So. Do you – Cam?

CAMERON   I – I – don't want my mother to, to know more than...

RUTH   I know, I know. I understand. Please help us then.

Camera: under the table. CAMERON*'s left hand is clasping his right wrist.*

CAMERON   I –

RUTH   Yes?

Silence.

Above the table CAMERON *appears motionless, but below...*

Camera: ever so slowly, his left hand moves to his right wrist as if to rub it again, but instead he begins to gently pull a rope from out of his sleeve.

(*Continues, unaware.*) Can we still find her in time? Is Joanna still alive?

Camera: the rope is being slowly wrapped around CAMERON*'s hands. He is staring at her.*

Her family deserve to know for sure. Even if it's the worst news, it's better than not knowing. The smallest chance she might somehow come home gnaws at people forever. But you can help them. Stop them being torn apart by that uncertainty... Will you at least save them from that?

Camera: the rope is wrapped around one hand and he begins to slowly wrap it around the other.

Cam. I know your mind must be spinning out right now, but try to listen to me...

Whatever you've done can't be changed. It's happened. But you can be in control of what happens now. You can help us resolve this quickly. Or you choose not to, and we have to go through each official step of the warrant, searching, interviews. Either way we get to the same result. But you can be in control of how this looks. How this looks to everyone, to people you know, to your mother. So your

mother can see that you helped us bring
Joanna home. Will you do that for me, Cam?

*Camera: the rope is taut between his
clenched fists. Then the shot cuts to –*

Camera: overhead shot.

All we can see is RUTH *and* CAMERON
staring at one another.

CAMERON   Can I – Can I have a – water?

RUTH   A water?

She glances over to the water cooler.

CAMERON   Yes.

RUTH *stays still.*

Please.

RUTH *gets up and turns her back to*
CAMERON. *As she approaches the water
cooler, he brings the rope to the table, looks
at her but stays seated.* RUTH *turns and sees
the rope. Stillness.*

(*Calmly, quietly.*) This is what you're looking
for.

CAMERON *unfurls the rope from his fists
and lets it fall onto the table. He sits back
into into his chair. Head back, eyes looking
up to the ceiling.*

RUTH *doesn't move from where she is.*
CAMERON *looks at her, then to the rope,
then pushes the rope away from himself to the
far-side of the table. Out of his reach.*

Do you have a map?

RUTH   Uh, a, uh, of where?

CAMERON   The area between Lambourn and Streatley.

RUTH	Yep, I should. In here.

She sits back down, looks through her folder and finds a map and pushes it across the table to him.

CAMERON	Thank you.

He studies the map closely as RUTH *stares at the rope.*

Here. Half a mile along from the roundabout. On the right. There's a sort of broken gate and a side road. Along the field. Drive a hundred and fifty yards or so, there's a slope. Down that. Under this big bracken-y hedge. She's there.

RUTH	Joanna?
CAMERON	Yeah. J– She's there.
RUTH	And she's…
CAMERON	Dead, yes.

RUTH *exhales.*

RUTH	Is she clothed?
CAMERON	Mostly. I tucked her up under a blanket.
RUTH	Right.
CAMERON	I was going to go back once everything quietened down. To give her a proper burial.
RUTH	When we, we find Joanna did you – do anything to her?
CAMERON	No, not sexual. Nothing like that.
RUTH	Okay.
CAMERON	I would never do anything like that.
RUTH	Okay.

CAMERON   I'm not twisted like that.

RUTH   And this – (*Indicating the rope.*)

CAMERON   It's what I used.

RUTH   You – you brought it here?

CAMERON   I always have it. With me. Most days. It
               feels – good.

RUTH   And how was there none of your DNA at
               Joanna's?

CAMERON   Was clever.

RUTH   Okay.

CAMERON   Gloves, mask, burnt clothes after. I did
               everything right.

RUTH   Thank you, Cam. You've done the good thing
               here. You've done really well. What happens
               now is that I –

CAMERON   You know –

RUTH   Yes?

CAMERON   Weeks after Vicky, I thought each call, every
               knock on the door was going to be your lot.
               But nothing. Nothing.

               And after that, I knew that I could do
               anything I liked. I could, I could brick
               someone sleeping in a doorway. Then walk
               down the road spattered red, and everyone
               would assume I'm doing whatever I'm doing
               because I should be. No questions asked...

               Silence.

RUTH   Cam.

               CAMERON*'s eyes are down and he doesn't
               respond.*

               Were Vicky and Joanna the only two?

CAMERON*'s eyes are down. A grunt of something that could be confirmation...*

What was that, Camero– I mean Cam?

CAMERON	(*Looking up.*) I – that's all I want to talk about for now.
RUTH	Okay. But –
CAMERON	That's all I have to say. Right now.
RUTH	Sure. Okay, you're doing well here, Cam, really well.

Silence.

Do you think it might have happened again?

CAMERON	I have no idea. If I thought it was best, then... If I needed to, then... probably. I had no reason not to.
RUTH	Okay.
CAMERON	I had nothing against any of these women. They were just there and looked right.
RUTH	Did they remind you of someone?
CAMERON	(*Stares, then.*) Breakfast was more bearable. With her. The next morning.

Silence.

I don't seem like the type. To do this sort of thing. Do I?

RUTH	To me, you do.
CAMERON	I imagine I won't be heading home tonight?

RUTH *shakes her head.*

Mother will have to cook for herself then. Will you let her know?

RUTH	Of course.

CAMERON	Thank you. Is this when you...? (*Shows wrists*.)
RUTH	Not me, but you'll be taken down the hall and read the charges in full for the abduction and murders of Vicky Edwards and Joanna Nelson.
CAMERON	Alright. Yes, well. Your father would be very proud of his little girl today, I'm sure.
	Beat, then –
RUTH	My dad isn't a security guard by the way. He never pushed me to do anything I didn't want to. And he was happy when I broke off my engagement with Mikey because Mikey was a prick.
CAMERON	(*Impressed*.) Huh. You know, I'm glad it was someone like you, Ruth. Sharper than you first pretended. Playing the rookie. That's what you were doing, wasn't it?
RUTH	Yep, I was.
CAMERON	Was that your idea?
RUTH	No.
CAMERON	And to talk to me by yourself?
RUTH	Uh –
CAMERON	His too?
RUTH	...
CAMERON	You alone. With me. Smart idea. Bait on a hook.
RUTH	...
CAMERON	And making you take off your ring?
RUTH	...
CAMERON	What a clever man.

RUTH   ...

CAMERON   Well, it was nice to meet you, DC Palmer. In a way.

              RUTH turns and knocks on the door twice.

              Keep those eyes peeled.

              The door opens and CAMERON is led away.

              RUTH looks up at the overhead camera, and finally turns it off.

              She exhales, then slumps into a chair.

              A moment. Then, JOHN steps, cautiously, into the room.

JOHN   Ehhh. There she is...

RUTH   ...

JOHN   (*Uncertainly.*) Congratulations! I knew it. I fucking knew it. What a star. That was... unlike you.

RUTH   ...

JOHN   'Security guard dad' – how'd you come up with something like that?

RUTH   Just came to me.

JOHN   What a blinder. 'Security guard dad.' Smarter than you look, Ruth. Right. We've sent the team to find the body and if she's there then that's us all wrapped up. Then we can shove that letter back to that MP prick and rub that smug –

RUTH   John – why did you have me do this by myself?

JOHN   Because I think you're brilliant and I was right, wasn't I?

RUTH	He had the fucking rope on him.
JOHN	That. Yeah, the scanners must'n've – yeah, that was a fuck-up. I mean, you were the one hurrying it along, but, we were down the corridor. Nothing could have happened.
RUTH	If he'd gone for me –
JOHN	Ruth.
RUTH	– no one could've got here before –
JOHN	Ruth.
RUTH	– he got that thing around my neck –
JOHN	Stop flapping!

Beat.

It may not have been pretty, but we got there in the end. You got us there. We have a way of doing things around here, and you have to trust us. Trust me. Every officer on the force is on the same team, fighting the good fight. Never forget that.

RUTH *nods*.

Good. Now let's get going.

RUTH	I thought I was interviewing him alone cos you thought I was good, not because I was bait.
JOHN	Ruth, I heard what he said. At the end there. And come on? You think I'd do that? Look at me.

RUTH *stares at him*.

I'm not that kind of guy, am I?

RUTH	(*Considering, then.*) No, no of course not.
JOHN	He was just trying to get into your head.

RUTH   I know.

JOHN   I've got your back. I'll always have your
            back.

RUTH   Yep, I know.

JOHN   Team-mates?

RUTH   Yep.

JOHN   Good. You smashed this.

            RUTH *just looks at him.*

            You know you can smile!

            RUTH *obliges. But it's as if something has*
            shifted between them.

            There she is. Come on. Grab your coat. We'll
            swing by to check the body, and then let's
            head out for a drink. See ya outside?

RUTH   Yep. See you.

            JOHN *exits.* RUTH *stares after him. Then*
            she looks down at her police lanyard, pulls it
            off, and holds it for a moment above the table
            deciding whether to –

            Blackout.

A Nick Hern Book

An Interrogation first published in Great Britain in 2025 as a paperback original by Nick Hern Books Limited, The Glasshouse, 49a Goldhawk Road, London W12 8QP

An Interrogation copyright © 2025 Jamie Armitage

Jamie Armitage has asserted his moral right to be identified as the author of this work

Cover image: Rebecca Pitt

Designed and typeset by Nick Hern Books, London
Printed in the UK by Mimeo Ltd, Huntingdon, Cambridgeshire PE29 6XX

A CIP catalogue record for this book is available from the British Library

ISBN 978 1 83904 416 8

www.nickhernbooks.co.uk/environmental-policy